A CROSSING OF ZEBRAS

Animal Packs in Poetry

Marjorie Maddox

Illustrations by Philip Huber

Honesdale, Pennsylvania

For my children, Anna Lee and Will, this *safari of poems*
— *M.M.*

To Gulia and Bella Faye Huber
—*P.H.*

Acknowledgments

Many thanks to the director of the Pennsylvania Center for the Book, Steven Herb, an enthusiastic advocate for children's literature and the first to encourage me to write for young readers; to Stephen Roxburgh and Joan Hyman at Boyds Mills Press for their editorial guidance; and to my mother, Roberta Scurlock, for her steadfast support. I am grateful to Lock Haven University for a sabbatical leave that allowed me to revise this work and also to a collection of librarians—especially Ted Nesbitt at West Liberty State College and Elsa Winch at Lock Haven University—for their helpful research. Most especially, I am indebted to my husband, Gary R. Hafer, faithful first reader and best friend.

— *M.M.*

Special thanks to my entire family for their love, support, and help with this book. Also, to Murray Tinkelman, who taught me to love every line.

—*P.H.*

Wordsong
An Imprint of Boyds Mills Press, Inc.
815 Church Street
Honesdale, Pennsylvania 18431
Printed in China

Based on an original concept by Philip Huber.

Library of Congress Cataloging-in-Publication Data

Maddox, Marjorie.
  A crossing of zebras : animal packs in poetry / Marjorie Maddox ; illustrations by Philip Huber.
    p. cm.
  ISBN 978-1-59078-510-2 (hardcover : alk. paper)
  1. Animals—Juvenile poetry. 2. English language—Collective nouns—Juvenile poetry. 3. Children's poetry, American. I. Huber, Philip, ill. II. Title.
  PS3613.A284324C76 2008
  811'.6—dc22
                                    2007031890

First edition
The text of this book is set in 13-point Caxton.
The illustrations are done in scratchboard with colored inks.

10 9 8 7 6 5 4 3 2 1

CONTENTS

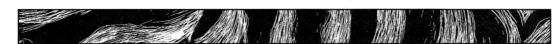

A Rumba of Rattlesnakes

A rumba of rattlesnakes knows how to shake
their long, slinky bodies and twist till daybreak.
They wobble their heads, give their hips a quick quake.
They jitterbug tails till their skeletons ache.

They rattle maracas and *rat-tat* on drums,
blow on tin trumpets, uncurl their tongues
to hiss a sweet song that invites you to come
a little bit closer. But you know to run

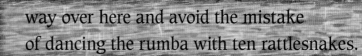

way over here and avoid the mistake
of dancing the rumba with ten rattlesnakes.

A TOWER OF GIRAFFES

Stacked high and wide,
please don't look down.
It's hard for you
to see the ground.
Look straight ahead
or else you're bound
to topple upside
down—your brown-
and-yellow legs
this way and that,
your long necks flat
upon the grass.
Take my advice:
don't try to chat
about the back-
flips coming next.
You'll hear us clap;
the crowd will roar.
Then that's the time
to show us more.

A Pounce of
Alley Cats

A pounce of alley cats, a city wall—
ferocious felines waiting for a brawl
(old, young, fat, thin, tall, furry, oh so small).
Beneath the bright streetlight, their shadows fall
on crumbling bricks. Their spooky shapes loom large
with high-arched backs and wide-stretched opened jaws.

Alas, here comes a neighbor's cuddly dog,
an unleashed puppy, hunting what he's lost,
a trotting spaniel—blind to nearly all
but buried bones and chewed-up rubber balls.
Be careful, canine, better move those paws.
When alley cats attack—kung fu with claws!

An Army of Ants

Army of ants, you step left-right, left-right;
with swords and spears, you ready for the fight.

Left-right, left-right: you drum a wartime beat,
salute with confidence, combat defeat

until you trample on OUR picnic spread,
invade our lemonade, our pumpkin bread,

and battle us for Grandma's shoofly pie.
"Release our captured crumbs or else you die!"

we holler after all your tiny feet—
but this time you march quickly in retreat.

A Murder of Crows

Oh no, there they go, a murder of crows
throwing corncobs at the tattered scarecrow.
Though they never quite hit her, they flap to and fro,
cawing and jawing out names as they go.
They eat what's not theirs, then rush back for more,
ignoring her warnings, her pleas for reform.
No polite songsters here, well mannered with charm,
just fast flying hoodlums unfit for a farm.

A Cartload of Monkeys

A cartload of monkeys bumptiously
bumbled and tumbled, looking for fleas.
One knocked his head; another, his knees,
stuck in that cart with no room to breathe.

Two flipped upside down, then fell in the mud.
(One's name was Lucy; the other's was Bud.)
All twenty-two monkeys wanted more grub
and wanted it now; they fought and they tugged.

They picked at each other, downed roaches and slugs
till all of those monkeys ate all of those bugs,
including twelve hundred and fifty-three fleas—
that's what one monkey confided to me!

A Leap of Leopards

bouncing,

hurdled high,

A leap of leopards

pouncing.

Stopping their hopping, frogs

dropped their

jaws.

They'd only dreamed such lofty rides,

hid their froggy heads to cry.

The leopards rasped, "Hey, there's room

to learn.

Practice your   jump.

Perfect your

ZOOOOOOOOOOOOOOOOOOOOOOOOOOM!"

Their green friends grinned, croaked out a tune,

leapfrogged and somer-
saulted

toward the moon.

A SCHOOL OF FISH

A school of fish reads in my swimming pool,
reciting ABCs and golden rules
(look both ways, be nice, no ocean duels).
They know it all—mountains to molecules:
T. rex, magic, Minotaurs, toadstools,
volcanoes, vipers, tricks for April Fool's,
Egyptian mummies, pirates and their jewels,
strange flying saucers, robots, ghosts and ghouls.
Their dictionaries float, Old Mother Goose
quacks her rhymes and rhythms; it's so cool
I'm signing a petition at *my* school—
let's hold class every summer at the pool.

A Crossing of Zebras

A crossing of zebras zigzags left to right
              then right to left. It's really a delight
           to watch their fancy footwork, hooves in flight.
       You first see white-and-black, then black-and-white
except, of course, if it's a moonless night,
        in which case you see only black-and-black.
              What can I say? I'm giving you the facts
                  in black-and-white.

A Band of Coyotes

A band of coyotes,
       hey, man,
             jams
guitars
        it's electric   drums

    horns   *psychedelic*
                saxophones
   talking 'bout my generation

Guthrie   *like, peace*   Joplin
      Mitchell
              back to the garden
    Hendrix
hear it   *dance*
      to the music
            tie-dyed
               bandannas
Oh yeah!
       and vans
         fueled by
     flower power

    with a little help from my friends
              again
     love
        not war
strawberry fields forever

A Scurry of Squirrels

They're tricksters at the county fair,
this scurry of squirrels.
Acrobats extraordinaire,
they dare each other to scare
      woodchucks waddling with balloons,
      a fox hawking his wares,
      a long-necked goose
      nibbling cupcakes with a bear,
      quails strolling with a loon,
      swallows swishing, rabbits twitching,
      cats sniffing the country air.
There's trouble here. Beware.
Mischief-makers at the fair,
take back your double-dare and share,
O scurry of squirrels!

A Pride of Lions

A pride of lions: glory shining,
regal cats no one can stop,
never shaggy, ever bragging,
stately lords of mountaintops.

Prowling, growling, boasting, gloating,
"We're the sharpest of the lot!"
Sleek and mighty, quickly spying
every secret jungle spot.

They're the kings of leaping, hiding—
tricky cats that can't be caught.
When they smell those hunters coming,
first they're here, and then   they're not!

A Crash of Rhinos

A crash of rhinos, scrambling here and there,
collides on parks and playgrounds—don't be scared.
Some skin-the-cat, while others hang midair
on monkey bars. In awe, the others stare.

They clamber up the jungle gym, or glide
up high on swings, play tag and seek-and-hide.
Then one by one, they line up for a ride
down the playground's tallest slippery slide.

Clash, *bash*, and *bam*—they pile up in tens,
reclimb the ladder steps, then bump again.
Wham, *wow*, and *pow*—they slam into their friends,
this crash of rhinos, smashing till the end.

A CHARM OF BUTTERFLIES

A charm of butterflies arrives each spring
and circles my backyard with rainbow wings.
I want to catch the beauty each one brings
and spread their joy to other living things.

Let's write a poem together. Yes, let's try
to re-create the charm of butterflies.
Let's celebrate in song. Let's dance their flight
and paint the way their wings reflect the light.

And later, when the trees are dark and bare,
we'll still have lots of butterflies to share.

A Note from the Author

Collective nouns—words that describe groups of animals, individuals, or things—have been around for centuries. Derived from both oral and written traditions, these words ignite our imaginations. They appeal to our playful sides. It's just plain fun to say *a gaggle of geese*.

But there's more here than first greets the ear. Many of the words' originators combined sound *and* meaning. There's solid knowledge packed in such tongue-tempting phrases as *a leap of leopards*, *a true love of turtledoves*, *a tower of giraffes*, *an unkindness of ravens*, and *a nest of rabbits*. Each gives us a glimpse of the animal's life.

As a lover of words, I couldn't help but consult, as some call themselves, *a collection of librarians*. With some diligent sleuthing, Ted Nesbitt, a research instructor at West Liberty State College in West Virginia, helped me track down the origins of *cage*, *box*, *barrel*, *bushel*, *bag*, and *cartload of monkeys*. In this book, *A Crossing of Zebras*, Philip Huber chose to illustrate *cartload*, prompted by the 1930 and 1968 expressions *clever as a cartload of monkeys* and *artful as a cartload of monkeys*.

Sometimes, though, the collective noun evolved from someone's mistake. This is what happened with the phrase *a school of fish*. For many of us, the words conjure a group of spectacle-donning carp grasping dictionaries with their fins, but that's not where the phrase started. The *Dictionary of Word Origins* tells us this collective noun comes from the prehistoric West Germanic word *skulo*. Later, this became the Middle Dutch word *schōle*— a "troop" of fish—and the English hunting term *shoal*—a large group. How did we end up with *school*? Hundreds of years ago, manuscripts were copied by hand and—at various points—scribes made mistakes. The errors stuck!

Authors, journalists, and animal enthusiasts continue to create these fun-to-say phrases. Realizing there was no official expression for butterflies, the North American Butterfly Association asked its members to suggest one. Abracadabra! *A charm of butterflies* flew in! Contemporary Web sites showcase lists that include *an army of ants*, *a band of coyotes*, and *a crossing of zebras*. Perhaps the latter evolved from the term *zebra crossing*, the street crosswalk marked with black-and-white stripes. The *Van Wert Daily Bulletin*, a small-town Ohio newspaper, reported in 1916 that the crossings on the Pennsylvania Railroad were "black and white in stripes." The *Oxford English Dictionary* lists several later references to *zebra crossings*. From these, did the phrase *a crossing of zebras* cross someone's thoughts? It's possible.

As you read through *A Crossing of Zebras*, I hope what will cross your thoughts are delightfully new ways to imagine this ever-changing world.

—*Marjorie Maddox*

For further exploration into the world of collective nouns, take a look at the following books and Web sites*:

Ayto, John. *Dictionary of Word Origins*. New York: Arcade Publishing, 1991.

Collings, Rex. *A Crash of Rhinoceroses: A Dictionary of Collective Nouns*. Wakefield, RI: Moyer Bell, 1993.

Heller, Ruth. *A Cache of Jewels and Other Collective Nouns*. New York: Grosset and Dunlap, 1987.

Lipton, James. *An Exaltation of Larks: The Ultimate Edition*. New York: Penguin Books, 1991.

Sparkes, Ivan G., ed. *Dictionary of Collective Nouns and Group Terms*. Detroit: Gale Research, 1983.

The Armchair Grammarian. community-2.webtv.net/solis-boo/Collectives/

Melissa Kaplan's Beastly Garden of Wordy Delights. www.anapsid.org/beastly.html

Oxford English Dictionary. www.askoxford.com/asktheexperts/collective/?view=uk

U.S. Geological Survey. www.npwrc.usgs.gov/about/faqs/animals/names.htm

*Active at time of publication